ELFABET
An ABC of Elves

◆ ◆ ◆

by JANE YOLEN

Illustrated by LAUREN MILLS

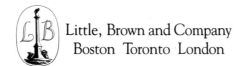
Little, Brown and Company
Boston Toronto London

Text copyright © 1990 by Jane Yolen
Illustrations copyright © 1990 by Lauren A. Mills

First edition

Library of Congress Cataloging-in-Publication Data

Yolen, Jane.
    Elfabet: an ABC of elves / by Jane Yolen; illustrated by Lauren
Mills. — 1st ed.
        p.   cm.
    Summary: Each letter of the alphabet is represented by a busy elf,
engaged in an alphabetically appropriate activity and surrounded by
objects beginning with the same letter.
    ISBN 0-316-96900-1
    1. Elves—Juvenile literature. 2. English language—Alphabet—
Juvenile literature. [1. Elves. 2. Alphabet.] I. Mills, Lauren
A., ill. II. Title.
GR549.Y65 1989
[E]—dc19   88-13494
                                                                    CIP
                                                                     AC

Illustrations done in watercolor ten percent larger than the
printed piece
Color separations made by Princeton Polychrome
Alphabet letters painted by the artist based on Goudy Catalogue
Text set in Goudy Old Style by Litho Composition Company, Inc.

10 9 8 7 6 5 4 3 2 1

HR

Published simultaneously in Canada
by Little, Brown & Company (Canada) Limited

Printed in the United States of America

For Maria, marvelously Modugno

J. Y.

Doodles deliriously dedicated to Dennis

L. M.

A is for Acorn Elf always acrobatic.

B is for Bottle Elf boldly balancing.

C is for Candle Elf carefully cooking.

D is for Dandelion Elf daintily dancing.

E is for Egg Elf endlessly eating.

F is for Feather Elf fearlessly flying.

G is for Grape Elf grumpily gathering.

H is for Honey Elf hopefully harvesting.

I is for Ice Elf idly inking.

J is for Jelly Elf joyfully jumping.

K is for Kite Elf keenly kicking.

L

1

Dear Lucy,
Here is another lollipop
for you. Let's hope that lazy
little elf won't find it first.
Love, Pops

BOSTON MA
02108
PM
13 JUNE 1989

L is for Lollipop Elf lazily licking.

M is for Mirror Elf merrily mimicking.

N is for Needle Elf neatly numbering.

O is for Orange Elf often overflowing.

P is for Paper Elf playfully parachuting.

Q is for Quilt Elf quietly quivering.

R is for Rose Elf restfully reading.

S is for Seashell Elf swiftly sliding.

T is for Tinsel Elf terribly tangled.

U is for Umbrella Elf usually upside down.

V is for Valentine Elf vigorously vaulting.

W is for Water Elf wearily washing.

X is for Xylophone Elf eXcitedly eXercising.

Y is for Yo-yo Elf youthfully yodeling.

Z is for Zipper Elf zestfully zigzagging.

KEY

A
acorns, ant, apple,
apple blossoms
in border: aardvark, alligator,
alpine asters

B
banjo, basil leaves, beetle,
bell, blouse, blue jeans, bottle,
bows, boysenberries, branch,
braids, bubbles, bumblebee,
buttercups, butterfly, buttons
in border: bear, bellflowers,
blackbird

C
cake, candle, checkered cloth,
chef's cap, cherries, cherry
blossoms, cows, cricket, cup
in border: cat, chick, chicken,
crocuses

D
dandelions, dice, domino,
dragonfly
in border: daisies,
dog (dalmatian), duck

E
eggshell, elderberries,
elder tree branch
in border: eagle, elephant,
evening primroses

F
feathers, figs, fig branch,
flower garland
in border: flamingo, frog,
fuchsias

G
gardening gloves, grapes,
grasshopper
in border: geraniums, giraffe,
goose

H
honey bees, honeycomb,
honey dipper, honey jars,
honeysuckle hat
in border: hamster, hedgehog,
hyacinths

I
ice, ice skates, ink,
ink berries, ink pen, inkwell
in border: iguana, impala, irises

J
jacks, jar, jasmine, jester suit,
jujube jelly
in border: jackal,
Jacob's ladders, jaguar

K
katydid, key, kimono,
kite, knots
in border: kangaroos,
king's spears, koala

L
ladybugs, letter, lizard,
lollipop, lotus, lotus position
in border: lilies, lion, lobster

M
marbles, millipede, mirror,
mistletoe, moth
in border: macaw, marigolds,
mouse

N
needle, nest, numbers, nut
in border: narcissus,
nightingale, nuthatch

O
olives, orange, orange blossoms,
orange juice
in border: okapi, oleanders, oriole

P
paper popper, paper streamers,
parachute, peace sign, peach,
pierrot suit
in border: panda, peacock,
poppies

Q
queen bee, quilt, quince,
quince blossoms
in border: quail,
Queen Anne's lace, quetzal

R

robin, rose, ruby ring
in border: rabbit, raccoon,
ragged robin

S

sand, sand dollar, scallop,
sea lavender, seashells,
sea snail, sea urchin, starfish,
stripes
in border: seahorse,
snapdragons, sparrow

T

teacup, tinsel, toad, toadstool,
toe shoes, top, toy truck, tree
branches, trumpet, tulips
in border: thistles, tiger, turtle

U

ukulele, umbrellas,
umbrella tree branches, utensils
in border: umbrella bird,
unicorn, uvularia

V

valentine, velvet, vine
in border: vicuña, violets, vole

W

washcloth, wasp, water,
watering can, water lilies,
water rat
in border: wallflowers, warthog,
woodpecker

X

xebec, xyleborus beetles,
xylophone
in border: xantusidae lizards,
xyridaceae

Y

yellow jacket,
yellow striped socks,
yew tree branch, yin-yang sign,
yo-yo
in border: yak, yarrows,
yellowthroat

Z

zephyr cloth, zipper, zodiac
in border: zebra, zebu, zinnias